LEADING WITH RESPECT

A Practical Guide to Fostering a Positive Workplace Culture

Phill Akinwale, OPM3, PMP

PUBLISHER

Praizion Media

Praizion Media

Real World Project Management Training Solutions

LEADING WITH RESPECT
Published by Praizion Media
P.O Box 22241, Mesa, AZ 85277
E-mail: info@praizion.com
www.praizion.com

Author
Phillip Akinwale, MSc, OPM3, PMP

ISBN 978-1-934579-39-8

The author and publisher have diligently worked to ensure the accuracy and completeness of the contents within this publication. However, they do not guarantee the applicability of the material for any specific purpose, including but not limited to passing any certification exams or professional qualifications. The information provided is intended to serve as a guide and should be used in conjunction with other relevant resources and best practices.
The author and publisher disclaim all responsibility for any losses, damages, or claims that may arise from the use of this publication, whether directly or indirectly. Users of this publication are encouraged to exercise their own judgment and consult with appropriate professionals when necessary.

Printed in the United States of America

Table of Contents

Business Case for This Book

Respect is the unsung hero of the workplace, a critical pillar that supports everything from project management to daily interactions. Despite its importance, highlighted by the PMI's Code of Ethics and Professional Conduct, we often overlook the nuances of giving and receiving respect. Are we really investing enough effort in understanding respect, not just in theory but in practice? Are we actively teaching, showing, and embodying what it means to respect our colleagues, our work, and ourselves?

Respect goes beyond simple manners. It's about the soft skills we're constantly evolving: clear communication, really listening to what others are saying, reading the room, showing patience, and a host of other abilities that don't always get the spotlight. When any of these elements falter, it can throw off our respect game.

Think about it: respecting others isn't just about knowing the rules; it's about feeling the rhythm of human interaction and acting accordingly. Ever caught yourself changing your approach when speaking to someone from a different age group or cultural background, just to make sure you're connecting respectfully? That's respect in action. It's about adapting to the context, being culturally savvy, especially when stepping into new or diverse environments. Some places can be pretty strict with their respect protocol – mess up, and you might not get a second chance.

I've learned to double down on respect whenever there's a hint of doubt, ensuring my words, my look, my tone, and my gestures all line up with my intent. Respect isn't just deep; it's wide-ranging, touching every aspect of our interactions. And here's something else: when you extend respect, it often comes back to you in surprising ways, opening doors and building bridges you never knew existed.

Bringing it back to our turf, the workplace, respect can look different depending on where you are and who you're with. That's why we're tackling respect head-on, but keeping it flexible—think of this as your guide to mastering respect in a diverse world. Let's dial into this conversation, make it real, and figure out how to weave respect into the very fabric of our day-to-day professional lives, no matter where we are or who we're working with.

Introduction

> "I've learned that people will forget what you said, people will forget what you did, but people will never forget how you made them feel."
>
> Maya Angelou

Respect: The foundation of a healthy society

Respect is essential for a healthy society. It is the foundation of trust, cooperation, and mutual understanding. When people feel respected, they are more likely to be engaged, productive, and civic-minded. They are also less likely to engage in harmful behaviors such as absenteeism, dropped performance, crime, jealousy, malice, and even murder.

How disrespect causes bad behavior

Disrespect can lead to a variety of bad behaviors, including:

- Absenteeism: When people feel disrespected at work, they are more likely to call in sick or take unauthorized leave.

- Dropped performance: Disrespected employees are less likely to be motivated and engaged in their work, which can lead to decreased productivity and performance.

- Crime: Disrespect can lead to feelings of anger, resentment, and revenge, which can increase the likelihood of criminal behavior.

- Jealousy: Disrespect can make people feel insecure and threatened, which can lead to feelings of jealousy and malice.

- Malice: Disrespect can make people feel like they have nothing to lose, which can increase the likelihood of malicious behavior, such as vandalism or violence.

- Murder: In some cases, disrespect can escalate to the point of murder.

Statistics and examples

A study by the Society for Human Resource Management found that 70% of employees who quit their jobs do so because they feel disrespected. A study by the University of California, Berkeley found that students who feel disrespected by their teachers are more likely to engage in disruptive behavior and have lower academic achievement. A study by the Centers for Disease Control and Prevention found that people who have experienced disrespect are more likely to be victims of violence.

Here are some specific examples of how disrespect can lead to bad behavior:

- A student who is constantly belittled by their teacher may start to skip class or engage in disruptive behavior.

- An employee who is micromanaged and criticized by their boss may become disengaged and unproductive.

- A person who is constantly cut off and ignored in social situations may become resentful and isolated.

- A person who is subjected to racial or sexual harassment may feel angry and vengeful.

- A person who is bullied or humiliated may feel hopeless and suicidal.

Disrespect is a serious problem that can have a devastating impact on individuals and society as a whole. It is important to remember that everyone deserves to be treated with respect, regardless of their race, gender, sexual orientation, religion, or any other factor. When we create a culture of respect, we create a healthier and more productive society for everyone.

A Yearning Need for Respect

In the intricate tapestry of human interactions, the thread of respect weaves the fabric of harmonious societies. Respect, or the lack thereof, serves as a powerful catalyst that shapes not only individual experiences but the very essence of communities. The need for respect is not a mere nicety; it is an indispensable cornerstone of a flourishing and functional society. As we delve into the significance of respect, it becomes evident that its absence can set in motion a cascade of detrimental consequences, ranging from diminished workplace performance to the alarming specter of crime and violence.

The Ripple Effect of Disrespect:

Disrespect, like a toxin, permeates every facet of human existence, leaving behind a trail of destructive repercussions. Workplace dynamics, for instance, are profoundly impacted by the presence or absence of respect. According to studies conducted by leading organizations, a staggering percentage of employees report decreased job satisfaction and increased absenteeism when subjected to disrespectful treatment. The link between disrespect and diminished performance is not merely anecdotal; it's supported by concrete data that reveals a direct correlation between workplace respect and overall productivity.

From Envy to Malice:

Disrespect doesn't confine itself to the boundaries of the workplace; it spills over into personal relationships, breeding envy and malice. Statistics show that a significant number of interpersonal conflicts and strained relationships stem from disrespect. Jealousy, fueled by a lack of regard for one another, festers and gives rise to a toxic environment where cooperation becomes nearly impossible. This corrosive cocktail of emotions can lead to not only fractured relationships but also fuel criminal behavior in extreme cases.

The Dark Side: Crime and Violence:

Disturbingly, disrespect has been identified as a precursor to crime and violence in various studies. Instances of murder, assault, and other violent crimes often trace their roots back to a breakdown in basic human respect. It's a sobering reality that disrespect, if left unchecked, can escalate to catastrophic levels, leaving entire communities grappling with the aftermath.

Concrete Examples:

Consider real-world examples where the absence of respect has had profound societal implications. Communities torn apart by crime waves, workplaces marred by high turnover rates, and families fractured by interpersonal strife all share a common thread—a lack of respect. These examples underscore the urgency of addressing disrespect not merely as a social faux pas but as a fundamental threat to the well-being of individuals and society at large.

In this exploration of the need for respect, we embark on a journey to unravel the intricate connections between respectful interactions and the health of our communities. The evidence is clear: respect is not a mere courtesy; it is a linchpin that holds the delicate balance of society intact. As we navigate through the layers of this critical subject, it becomes increasingly apparent that fostering a culture of respect is not just a noble endeavor; it is an imperative for the collective welfare of humanity.

Chapter 1: Never Let it Get to You

> "No one can make you feel inferior without your consent."
>
> Eleanor Roosevelt

As a leader, the first and foremost key to earning respect is maintaining your composure. No matter the challenges, frustrations, or setbacks, resist the urge to let it get under your skin. A calm and collected leader sets the tone for the entire team, fostering an environment where respect can flourish.

Satya Nadella, Microsoft

In 2014, Satya Nadella took over as CEO of Microsoft during a time when the company was struggling to keep up with competition. Despite the pressure, Nadella consistently exhibited calm and composed leadership. He focused on changing the culture from one that was combative to one that was collaborative and rooted in a growth mindset. His composure under pressure helped to turn Microsoft around and re-establish it as a tech powerhouse.

1.1 The Composure of Leadership

"Keep your head when all about you are losing theirs." - Rudyard Kipling.

As a leader, you're the helm of your team's ship. In the stormiest of seas, it's your duty to maintain composure. Your reaction sets the stage for others to follow. If you exhibit frustration, your team will mirror it. If you stay calm, the team is likely to adopt a similar demeanor. A leader's composure is contagious; it's the bedrock upon which respect is built.

1.2 Emotional Intelligence in Practice

"Any person capable of angering you becomes your master." - Epictetus.

Emotional intelligence is your ally. Understand your emotions, triggers, and the strategies needed to remain poised. Reflect on what pushes your buttons and develop a game plan for those moments well in advance. This foresight will not only prevent knee-jerk reactions but will also cement your reputation as a leader who can't be easily shaken.

Chapter 1 Exercise: Never Let it Get to You

Physical Exercise: Stress-Reduction Techniques

1. Breathing exercises: Practice deep breathing techniques to maintain composure in stressful situations.

2. Role-playing: Simulate high-pressure scenarios and practice maintaining calm through physical posture and composed responses.

3. Yoga or meditation: Incorporate a regular practice to improve emotional regulation.

Debate Topic: The Impact of Leader's Emotion on Team Morale

Divide participants into two groups to debate the statement: "A leader's show of emotion in the workplace is more harmful than helpful."

Research Assignment: Study of Composure

Research prominent leaders who have faced public scrutiny and write a brief on how they maintained or lost composure, and the consequences of their reactions.

Observation Task: Reflective Journaling

Keep a daily journal for a week, noting any moments you felt challenged and how you responded, reflecting on what triggered emotional responses and how you might handle similar situations in the future.

Chapter 2: Remind Yourself Not to Let it

"The longer you dwell on your misfortunes, the greater their power to harm you."
- Voltaire.

It's easy to say "don't let it bother you," but it's another thing to consistently practice it. Remind yourself daily of the bigger picture, the goals you're working towards, and the positive impact you aim to make. By staying focused on the mission, you'll be better equipped to navigate challenges without letting them affect your leadership.

Howard Schultz, Starbucks

Howard Schultz, the CEO of Starbucks, faced significant backlash when the company's push into Australia failed. Instead of letting the criticism get to him, he used the experience as a learning opportunity. Schultz continually reminded himself and his team of the core mission of Starbucks, allowing them to rebound and expand more thoughtfully in other international markets.

2.1 The Power of Perspective

It's human nature to ruminate on the negative, but as a leader, you must practice the art of perspective. Each day, remind yourself of your goals, values, and the impact you wish to make. By focusing on these elements, you can navigate through adversity without losing your footing.

2.2 Cultivating Resilience

"Do not judge me by my successes, judge me by how many times I fell down and got back up again." - Nelson Mandela.

Resilience isn't a trait you're born with; it's a skill you develop. Each day is an opportunity to strengthen this muscle. Remind yourself of your past triumphs over adversity and use those victories to fuel your resilience in current and future challenges.

Chapter 2 Exercise: Remind Yourself Not to Let it Get to You

Physical Exercise: Mindfulness and Resilience Building

1. Mindfulness walking: Engage in a mindful walk, focusing on the environment to practice being present and not letting distractions affect you.

2. Stress ball use: Keep a stress ball at your desk and use it when feeling overwhelmed to remind yourself to stay calm.

3. Resilience training: Participate in a workshop or online course to build resilience.

Debate Topic: The Power of Positive vs. Negative Reinforcement

Argue for or against the idea that positive reinforcement is more effective than negative reinforcement in maintaining a leader's focus and composure.

Research Assignment: Biographies of Resilient Leaders

Choose a biography of a leader known for their resilience and summarize the techniques they used to keep perspective during tough times.

Observation Task: Media Monitoring

Monitor and note how public figures handle criticism or stressful situations in the media over a period and analyze their methods for maintaining composure.

Chapter 3: Set Boundaries and Team Charters

> "Expectations are like fine pottery. The harder you hold them, the more likely they are to crack."
>
> - Brandon Sanderson.

Respect stems from clear expectations. Establish boundaries and team charters that clearly outline roles, responsibilities, and acceptable behavior. When everyone understands the rules of the game, it becomes easier to work together harmoniously, creating an atmosphere of mutual respect.

Anne Mulcahy, Xerox

When Anne Mulcahy became CEO of Xerox, the company was on the brink of bankruptcy. She established clear boundaries and expectations for her team, focusing on accountability and open communication. By setting these clear boundaries, she was able to lead a successful turnaround of the company, which returned to profitability under her leadership.

3.1 The Clarity of Expectations

Setting clear expectations is like drawing a map for a treasure hunt; it guides the team towards the desired destination. Use team charters to outline not just roles and responsibilities, but also the principles and ethics that define your team's culture. Clear boundaries are the guardrails that keep everyone on the path to success.

3.2 Respecting the Line

"Boundaries are to protect life, not to limit pleasures." - Edwin Louis Cole.

Boundaries should not be perceived as limitations, but as the defining lines that enable team members to work freely and creatively within a safe and respectful environment. They provide a clear understanding of where flexibility ends and non-negotiables begin.

Chapter 3 Exercise: Set Boundaries and Team Charters

Physical Exercise: Boundary-Setting Workshop

1. Role-play exercises: Practice setting boundaries in various scenarios, from simple to complex.

2. Creation of a team charter: Collaboratively draft a team charter that includes boundaries for behavior, communication, and work processes.

3. Assertiveness training: Engage in activities that improve assertive communication, essential for setting boundaries.

Debate Topic: Transparency vs. Privacy in Leadership

Debate the balance between being an open, transparent leader and maintaining a private, professional boundary with team members.

Research Assignment: Analyzing Successful Team Charters

Research and analyze team charters from successful companies to understand best practices in boundary-setting and expectations.

Observation Task: Boundary Effectiveness Assessment

Observe a team meeting or project group and note instances where clear boundaries aid in efficiency and where lack of them causes issues.

Chapter 4: Empower and Encourage

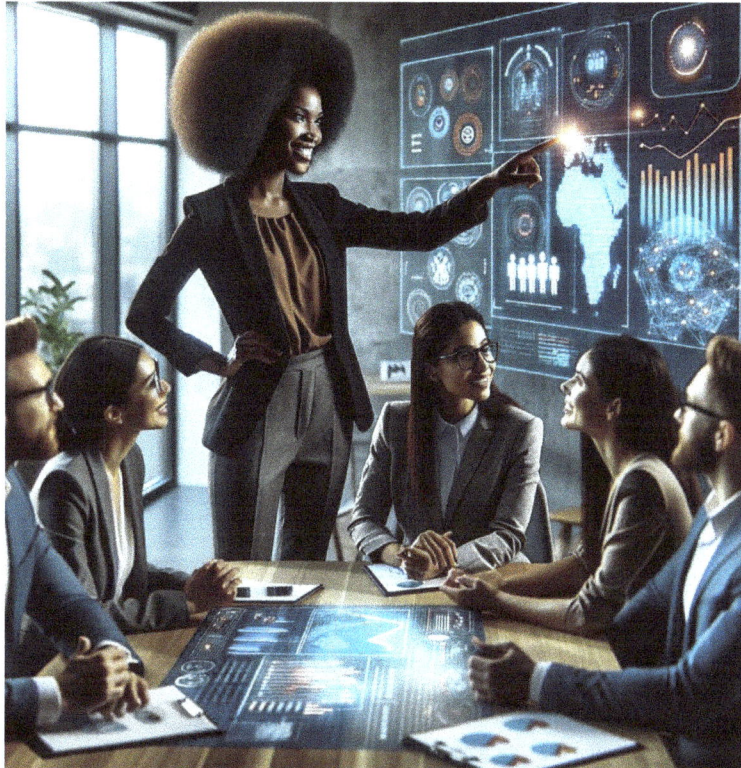

> "Leadership is not about being in charge. It's about taking care of those in your charge."
>
> - Simon Sinek

A respectful leader empowers their team members to take ownership of their work. Acknowledge their strengths, provide opportunities for growth, and celebrate achievements. A team that feels valued and encouraged is more likely to reciprocate that respect towards their leader and each other.

Ursula Burns, Xerox

As the first African American woman CEO of a Fortune 500 company, Ursula Burns is known for her empowering leadership style at Xerox. She encouraged her team to take ownership of their work and provided opportunities for employees to grow into leadership roles, which fostered a culture of respect and innovation within the company.

4.1 The Strength of Empowerment

When you empower your team, you give them the keys to unlock their potential. Provide them with the autonomy to make decisions and the confidence to act on their ideas. Empowerment fosters innovation and drives a team's commitment to shared goals.

4.2 Celebrating Each Milestone

"Don't wait for extraordinary opportunities. Seize common occasions and make them great." - Orison Swett Marden.

Recognition and encouragement are the fuels that drive people to keep pushing forward. Celebrate not only the major achievements but also the small victories. A simple acknowledgment can boost morale and reinforce the behaviors you want to see repeated.

Chapter 4 Exercise: Empower and Encourage

Physical Exercise: Leadership and Empowerment Activities

1. Trust falls: Build trust within the team through physical trust exercises like trust falls.

2. Problem-solving course: Set up a course with problems that teams can only solve by empowering each member to contribute.

3. Praise practice: Role-play giving specific, meaningful praise to empower and encourage peers.

Debate Topic: Autonomy vs. Micromanagement

Conduct a debate on whether a leader should empower team members with complete autonomy or if some level of micromanagement is necessary.

Research Assignment: Case Studies on Empowerment

Study cases of companies known for empowering their employees and present findings on the methods and outcomes of such practices.

Observation Task: Encouragement Audit

Observe a colleague for a day and record instances where they empower or encourage others, noting the impact on team dynamics.

Chapter 5: Coach, Mentor, and Train

"An organization's ability to learn, and translate that learning into action rapidly, is the ultimate competitive advantage."

-Jack Welch

Invest time in the development of your team members. Be a coach, offering guidance and constructive feedback. Serve as a mentor, sharing your experiences and insights. Prioritize continuous training to keep everyone at the top of their game. A leader committed to the growth of their team earns both admiration and respect.

Story: Eric Schmidt, Google

Eric Schmidt, when he was CEO of Google, played a significant role as a coach and mentor to founders Larry Page and Sergey Brin. He used his experience to guide them through the process of scaling the company while instilling a culture of continuous learning and innovation.

5.1 The Investment in Growth

"Leadership and learning are indispensable to each other." - John F. Kennedy.

As a leader, your role extends beyond management to coaching, mentoring, and training. By investing in the professional development of your team, you're not just enhancing their skills—you're demonstrating your belief in their potential. This investment is a testament to your commitment to their growth and to the success of the organization.

5.2 Continuous Learning as a Core Value

Embed the philosophy of continuous improvement into your team's culture. Encourage learning from every situation, and provide resources for ongoing education. When you prioritize growth, you build a team that is adaptable, skilled, and deeply respected.

Chapter 5 Exercise: Coach, Mentor, and Train

Physical Exercise: Coaching Role Play

1. Mentoring sessions: Pair up team members and have them conduct mock mentoring sessions on professional development topics.

2. Coaching clinic: Host a clinic where participants practice coaching each other on specific skills or tasks.

3. Training relay: Create a relay race where each station involves learning and then teaching a small task to the next person.

Debate Topic: The Effectiveness of Formal vs. Informal Training

Debate the merits and drawbacks of formal structured training programs versus informal, on-the-job training.

Research Assignment: Best Practices in Professional Development

Research best practices in coaching, mentoring, and training within the industry and compile a guidebook or presentation.

Observation Task: Peer Coaching Observation

Observe a coaching or mentoring session and analyze the techniques used by the coach or mentor to facilitate learning and growth.

Chapter 6: Allow for Margin of Error

> "To err is human; to forgive, divine."
>
> - Alexander Pope

Recognize that everyone is human and prone to making mistakes. Rather than immediately jumping to criticism, believe that your team is doing their best with the resources and information available. Cultivate an atmosphere that encourages learning from errors rather than dwelling on blame.

Reed Hastings, Netflix

Reed Hastings, CEO of Netflix, has fostered a company culture that allows for a margin of error. This was exemplified when Netflix decided to split its DVD and streaming services, a move that initially resulted in significant customer backlash. Instead of doubling down, Hastings acknowledged the mistake, reversed the decision, and learned from the experience, which has led to Netflix's continued evolution and success.

6.1 The Human Element of Leadership

Accepting that mistakes are part of the human experience is crucial. When errors occur, approach them with a mindset geared towards learning and improvement rather than punishment. This approach fosters trust and open communication, and your team will respect you for it.

6.2 Fostering a Culture of Innovation

"I have not failed. I've just found 10,000 ways that won't work." - Thomas A. Edison.

Innovation requires trial and error. Create an environment where team members are not paralyzed by the fear of making mistakes. Encourage experimentation and view each error as a step towards discovering a successful solution.

Chapter 6 Exercise: Allow for Margin of Error

Physical Exercise: Failure Workshops

1. Failure storytelling: Share personal stories of failure and the lessons learned in a group setting.

2. "Escape room" challenge: Engage in an "escape room" where mistakes are part of the problem-solving process.

3. Innovation sandbox: Create a safe space where team members can experiment with new ideas without fear of failure.

Debate Topic: Zero Tolerance vs. Learning from Mistakes

Debate whether a zero-tolerance policy on mistakes is more or less effective than a culture that encourages learning from errors.

Research Assignment: Innovators' Mistakes

Research famous innovators and the mistakes they made on the path to success and present how those mistakes were critical to their learning process.

Observation Task: Error Response Analysis

In a group setting, observe how team members respond to mistakes and note the outcomes of different approaches to handling errors.

Chapter 7: Retrospective - Audit - Reflect

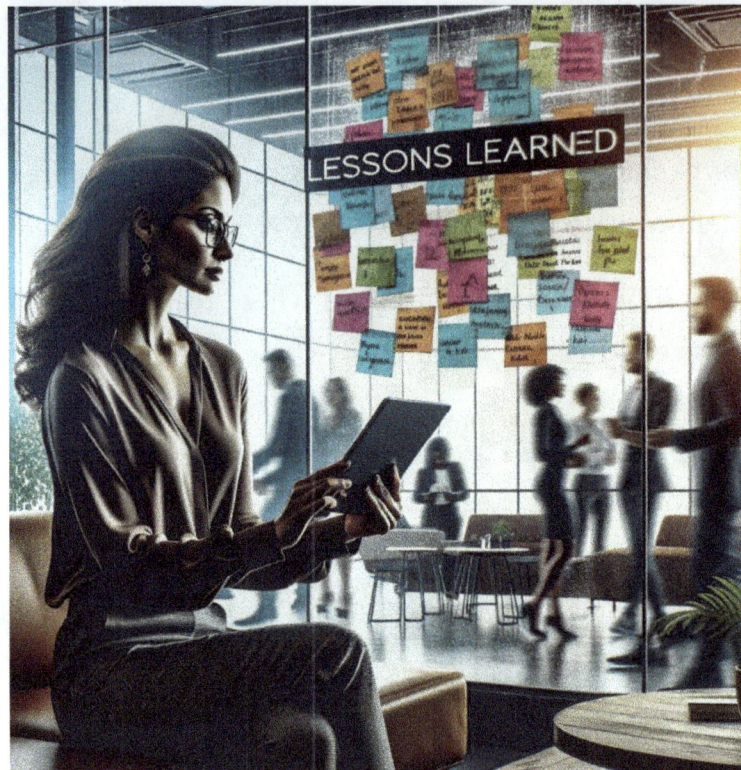

> *"Reflection turns experience into insight."*
>
> - John C. Maxwell

Regularly assess the team dynamics through retrospectives. Audit your leadership approach and the team's performance. Reflect on what worked well and what could be improved. This continuous feedback loop not only enhances the team's efficiency but also demonstrates your commitment to creating a respectful and evolving workplace.

Jeff Bezos, Amazon

Jeff Bezos is known for his retrospective approach at Amazon, often initiating high-quality audits and reflecting on the outcomes. This was evident in the development of the Kindle. Amazon's initial attempts at creating an e-reader were not successful, but through reflection and auditing their approach, they were able to innovate and create a product that transformed the industry.

7.1 The Reflective Leader

Regular retrospectives are a mirror for the team's progress and challenges. Use them to celebrate what went well and to dissect what didn't. Reflecting on these insights collectively paves the way for continuous improvement.

7.2 The Cycle of Improvement

"The only source of knowledge is experience." - Albert Einstein.

Auditing and reflecting should not be seen as a once-off event but as part of a continuous cycle of improvement. By regularly examining the team's dynamics and your leadership approach, you foster an environment that is not just respectful, but also dynamic and responsive to change.

Chapter 7 Exercise: Retrospective - Audit - Reflect

Physical Exercise: Reflection Exercises

1. Group meditation: Engage in a guided meditation focused on reflection of past actions and future intentions.

2. Reflection in motion: Take reflective walks post-project to discuss what went well and what didn't.

3. Role-reversal: Swap roles in a team to gain perspective on different responsibilities and challenges.

Debate Topic: The Value of Retrospectives

Hold a debate on whether regular retrospectives contribute to or hinder the momentum of a team.

Research Assignment: The Art of the Audit

Conduct research on different audit techniques that companies use to reflect on their processes and performance.

Observation Task: Self-Audit

Perform a self-audit on your own work over the past month, reflecting on successes, challenges, and areas for growth.

Conclusion

In the unfolding narrative of our professional lives, the chapters we've explored are more than mere guidelines; they are the foundational practices that, when woven into the very fabric of our daily interactions, can elevate the ordinary to the extraordinary. The pursuit of respect within the workplace is a journey, not a destination—a continuous process of learning, adapting, and growing.

As we close the pages of this exploration, remember that the art of respect is akin to a craft that requires patience, dedication, and consistent practice. It is an exercise in mindfulness, a commitment to stay present in the moment, to listen actively, and to engage authentically. In the fast-paced rhythm of our workdays, it's all too easy to lose sight of the impact our words and actions have on those around us. But by making a conscious effort to practice the principles of respect, empowerment, and understanding, we not only enhance our own leadership but also contribute to a culture of mutual respect that inspires others to follow suit.

The real world is our arena, and every interaction is an opportunity to practice the art of respect—to reinforce boundaries with compassion, to empower with integrity, and to learn from our missteps with grace. As leaders and colleagues, let us pledge to remain vigilant in our efforts, to encourage debate and reflection, and to embrace the diverse tapestry of humanity within our professional spheres.

May we always be mindful of the power of respect to unlock potential, to bridge divides, and to foster an environment where all are valued and heard. Let's carry forward the lessons learned, the insights gained, and the wisdom shared, knowing that each moment is a fresh chance to demonstrate respect, to enhance our workplace, and to perfect our practice of these timeless principles.

Let this conclusion not signify an end, but rather a new beginning—a call to action to persistently apply what we have discussed, to stay in the moment, and to continuously improve. For in the grand pursuit of creating a respectful workplace, our efforts today will shape the legacy of our leadership tomorrow.

Your Friend Phill

About the Author

Phill C. Akinwale, PMP, is a highly experienced project management professional with a proven track record in both government and private sectors. Throughout his career, he has worked with renowned companies such as Motorola, Honeywell, Emerson, Skillsoft, Citigroup, Iron Mountain, Brown and Caldwell, US Airways, and CVS Caremark, managing operational endeavors, projects, and project controls.

With his extensive knowledge and expertise in various facets of Project Management, Phill has become a trusted figure in the field. He has trained project management professionals worldwide, including prestigious organizations like NASA, FBI, USAF, USACE, US Army, and the Department of Transport. Over the past 15 years, he has provided training across five editions of the PMBOK® Guide, showcasing his commitment to staying up-to-date with industry standards.

Originally from a Civil Engineering (BEng) and Construction Information Technology (M.Sc.) background, Phill holds an impressive twelve project management certifications, with a notable focus on Agile Project Management. His certifications include Certified ScrumMaster (CSM), PMI Agile Certified Practitioner (PMI-ACP), Professional Scrum Master (PSM), Professional Scrum Product Owner (PSPO), Professional Agile Leadership (PAL), and Scaled Professional Scrum (SPS). This diverse range of certifications reflects his dedication to mastering various project management methodologies.

In addition to his project management expertise, Phill is a certified coach and speaker through the John Maxwell team. Leveraging his leadership and soft skills, he delivers impactful workshops, seminars, keynote speeches, and coaching sessions. He is passionate about guiding individuals, teams, and organizations in their desired direction, equipping them with the tools and knowledge to achieve their goals.

Phill is also a prolific author, having written over 20 books on a diverse range of topics. His written works cover areas such as bullying (including "The Bird Brained Bullies"), leadership, conflict resolution, time travel ("The Time Machine Project"), and even comics ("Project VBX 11"). Furthermore, he has created two short movies that explore themes of leadership drama in the workplace and project management.

With his vast experience, certifications, and passion for guiding others, Phill C. Akinwale, PMP, is a valuable asset to any organization or individual seeking agile coaching, project management expertise, leadership development, and personal growth.